MY FAVORITE
PRAYERS

Illustrations by Anna Láng

WSkids
WHITE STAR KIDS

PRAYERS ARE SPECIAL, PRECIOUS WORDS.

They retain an extraordinary power: they can trigger pure emotions within us and they connect us with the most enlightened part of our heart.

Through the power of words, we communicate with God and with our neighbor.

One by one, they build bridges and paths for us to walk throughout our life as Christians, because faith is a journey and each prayer guides us forward.

This book is your companion; it collects the most beautiful Christian prayers to help you move the first steps into this wonderful, life-changing journey.

My favorite Prayers

SIGN OF THE CROSS

In the name of the Father,
and of the Son,
and of the Holy Spirit.
Amen

HAIL MARY

Hail Mary, full of Grace,
the Lord is with Thee;
Blessed art Thou among women
and blessed is the fruit of Thy womb, Jesus.
Holy Mary, Mother of God,
Pray for us sinners now,
and at the hour of our death.
Amen

OUR FATHER

Our Father, who art in heaven;
hallowed be Thy name.
Thy kingdom come, Thy will be done
on earth as it is in Heaven.
Give us this day our daily bread,
and forgive us our trespasses
as we forgive those who trespass against us.
And lead us not into temptation;
but deliver us from evil.
Amen

ANGEL OF GOD

Angel of God,
My guardian dear,
To whom His love commits me here,
Ever this day be at my side,
To light and guard, to rule and guide.
Amen

ACT OF CONTRITION

O my God, I am heartily sorry for having offended Thee, and I detest all my sins because of Thy just punishments, but most of all because they offend Thee, my God, Who art all-good and deserving of all my love. I firmly resolve with the help of Thy grace to sin no more and to avoid the near occasions of sin.

DEAREST LORD,
TEACH ME

Dearest Lord,

teach me to be generous;

teach me to serve You as I should;

to give and not to count the cost,

to fight and not to heed the wounds,

to toil and not to seek for rest,

to labour and ask not for reward,

save that of knowing that I do Your most holy will.

MORNING PRAYER

Lord in the silence of this new day,

I ask you peace, wisdom and strength.

Today I want to look at the world with eyes of love.

Help me to be patient, understanding,

humble, gentle and good.

Please let me see others as you see them,

that I may look past appearances,

and appreciate the goodness in everyone.

Close my ears to all of the gossip,

and save my tongue from speaking evil of others.

Please let only thoughts that bless remain in me.

Today I want to be well-intentioned and fair,

that everybody that who comes to me might feel your presence.

Father, clothe me in your kindness,

that throughout this day I might be a reflection of you.

Amen

GRACE

Bless us, O Lord, and these, Thy gifts, which
we are about to receive from Thy bounty.
Through Christ, our Lord.
Amen

NIGHTTIME PRAYER

My God, I love You with all my heart. I thank You for having kept me safe this day. Pardon me the evil I have done and accept the good I have done. Take care of me while I sleep and deliver me from all danger. May Your grace be always with me and with all my loved ones. Amen

St. Augustine's Prayer to the Holy Spirit

Breathe in me, O Holy Spirit, that my thoughts may all be holy.

Act in me, O Holy Spirit, that my work, too, may be holy.

Draw my heart, O Holy Spirit, that I love but what is holy.

Strengthen me, O Holy Spirit, to defend all that is holy.

Guard me, then, O Holy Spirit, that I always may be holy.

Amen

Saint Augustine

THE APOSTLE'S CREED

I believe in God,
the Father almighty,
Creator of heaven and earth
I believe in Jesus Christ, His only Son, our Lord,
who was conceived by the Holy Spirit
and born of the Virgin Mary,
suffered under Pontius Pilate,
was crucified, died, and was buried;
He descended into hell;
on the third day He rose again from the dead;
He ascended into heaven,
and is seated at the right hand of God the Father Almighty;
from there He will come to judge the living and the dead.
I believe in the Holy Spirit,
the Holy Catholic Church,
the communion of Saints,
the forgiveness of sins,
the resurrection of the body,
and life everlasting.
Amen

THE MAGNIFICAT

My soul glorifies the Lord,

My spirit rejoices in God my Savior.

He looks on his servant in her lowliness;

Henceforth all generations will call me blessed.

The Almighty works marvels for me.

Holy his name!

His mercy is from age to age,

on those who fear him.

He puts forth his arm in strength

And scatters the proud hearted.

He casts the mighty from their thrones

And raises the lowly.

He fills the starving with good things,

Sends the rich away empty.

He protects Israel, his servant,

remembering his mercy,

the mercy promised to our fathers,

to Abraham and his sons for ever.

Glory be to the Father and to the Son and to the Holy Spirit,

as it was in the beginning, is now, and ever shall be, world without end.

Amen

HAIL, HOLY QUEEN

Hail, Holy Queen, Mother of mercy,
Hail our life, our sweetness and our hope!
To Thee do we cry, poor banished children of Eve.
To Thee do we send up our sighs, mourning and weeping
in this vale of tears! Turn, then, most gracious Advocate,
Thine eyes of mercy toward us,
and after this our exile,
show unto us the blessed fruit of Thy womb, Jesus.
O merciful, O loving,
O sweet Virgin Mary!

GLORY BE TO THE FATHER

Glory be to the Father
and to the Son,
and to the Holy Spirit,
as it was in the beginning,
is now and ever shall be,
world without end.
Amen

ACT OF LOVE

Oh my God,
I love you above all things,
with my whole heart and soul,
because you are all good and worthy of all my love.
I love my neighbor as myself for the love of you.
I forgive all who have injured me and I ask pardon
of all whom I have injured.

Prayer of
Saint Francis

Lord, make me an instrument of Your peace.

Where there is hatred, let me sow love;

Where there is injury, pardon;

Where there is doubt, faith;

Where there is despair, hope;

Where there is darkness, light.

Where there is sadness, joy.

O Divine Master,

grant that I may not so much seek

to be consoled as to console;

to be understood as to understand;

to be loved as to love.

For it is in giving that we receive;

it is in pardoning that we are pardoned;

it is in dying that we are born again to eternal life.

ANNA LÁNG

Anna Láng is a Hungarian graphic designer and illustrator who is currently living and working in Sardinia. After attending the Hungarian University of Fine Arts in Budapest, she graduated as a graphic designer in 2011. She worked for three years with an advertising agency, at the same time working with the National Theatre of Budapest. In 2013 she won the award of the city of Békéscsaba at the Hungarian Biennale of Graphic Design with her Shakespeare Poster series. At present she is working passionately on illustrations for children's books. In recent years she has brilliantly illustrated a number of titles for White Star Kids.

WS kids
WHITE STAR KIDS

White Star Kids® is a registered trademark property of White Star s.r.l.

© 2019, 2020 White Star s.r.l.
Piazzale Luigi Cadorna, 6
20123 Milan, Italy
www.whitestar.it

Revised edition

ISBN 978-88-544-1669-7
1 2 3 4 5 6   24 23 22 21 20

Printed in China